AARON WILLIAMSON

CATHEDRAL LUNG

For Melanie

Best wishes
& thanks.

[signature]

25/2/92.

CREATION PRESS

"CATHEDRAL LUNG"

by

Aaron Williamson

ISBN 1 871592 06 2

Published 1991 by
CREATION PRESS
83, Clerkenwell Road
London EC1
Tel 071 430 9878

"Freedom, liberty and tinsel"
was first published in 1989.

Front cover photo by Tertia Longmire

Photo of Aaron Williamson by
Adrian Franklin

CONTENTS

CATHEDRAL LUNG

In a room surrounded by at least two masochists, I have to try and shoot my way out says an imitation voice of what could be taken for god in an accelerating series of subtitles...

'I have to try and talk my way out'

Tongue
pulls along
pulleys, tarpaulins and traps
bolted to nets and levers
leaving
a grey-black hammer metallic
grease
          behind;
the whole thing
                    groaning
the whole thing
                    breathing ballast,
a snail slides towards daylight
tunnelling iron
into the roots;
winches hoisting the
dead mass of dead purple
weight
on to the silken weight
of lips that languish,
lying there,
                pululating ,
                    flicking

-and then it entered into my throat.

Reveal a black opening from the removal of a slab. Compressed gases steam forth, release an inner ichor and pulse the exhalations less. The pit again presents the tip of a flight of stone; unbearable. Lanterns ebb and flood against a thick-set effluence hovering the steps. Light glances the rim of horned black vegetation caked with niter and bordered by moist.

The utmost step is a salver offered up. One hand and two footprints indented. Unmarried, uncertain. Pools shaped by the prints dispense no light, no oiled windows for entry. Depthless, perhaps drilled, the palm and soles are surface rims of tubiforms; strata, rockwells brimming with cumulus.

Such gross luxuriance in this, the first lucid visitation of pausing alveoli; a revelation composed of carbonated entrances, the certainties of half-obliterated burdens. And these become apparent as the burdens of an absence: a mineshaft that is lessening as it attains substantiality.

And in this way, one recalls the cathedral lung, a site of worship; 'where the heavens do avidly aspire'; and in here is the point upon which the total axis is balanced: a hair trigger that is all but eaten away, a gnawed fibre that can be used to hurl aside the static swarm.

A sudden jolt. In the star light, the drifted earth surface, weeds and archaic grass. Alone. Amongst immense granite slabs. Survey the scene at length and then, inevitably, begin the mental calculations.

The jolt is sustained by the shadows which tremble. A lever lies near to a stony ruin; the central slab impacted into a violent clangour. The light slides away from a landscape which is nailed by its edges to a vacuum in space; a nadir invisible by dint of its omnipresence.

The combined strength of the atmosphere comes to its assistance, jibs off the light and seizes the lever. Finally and tipped to one side. The stone. Which it raised.

Reveal the cosmogenic intricacies of the cathedral.

Layers heave an internal web, dead wheels of fortune churn, in urgency, hysterical, a saffron sun in cycle with the trinities of freaks splashed out at intersecting grids and networks; writhing, flashing.

Molecules burn out. A substrate warm mosaic transforms the panic into optical sensations, these accompanied by manacled anguishes of suffocation.

Transparent grating sounds screeching impeccably. A thread of panes cross-sect precise disembodiments of frost as swollen developments of insects colonise the permeable clamour.

Inside the stellar vagus vault, the flayed tongue is painted with menstrual flake. A gong is pulverised.

The silence begins.

Voice 1:　　QUOTA COUNT TO PUNCTUATE
　　　　　　A TABERNACLE OUTBURST!

Voice 2:　　Obey, obey,

　　　1:　　APOPLEXY CUTICLE CAUSTIC
　　　　　　PICKABACK TOCCATA
　　　　　　TOECAP QUOTIENT ABORT

　　　2:　　ache, utter,
　　　　　　ache, utter,

　　　1:　　UPPITY TACK

　　　2:　　Take, cutter,

　　　1:　　CATATEPTIC BETA

　　　2:　　Pucker

　　　1:　　TATTY TAPE ABATE
　　　　　　ABBOT

　　　2:　　ache, utter,

　　　1:　　ACHE!

And this is how the mouth is
hoisted onto the body
in order to locate the position
of an absentee
who can but whisper the malevolence
of an eternal tinsel city.

Here stands
just one moment
within the life
of a monument.

Clouds clash!
a vast burgeoning
suctionlike
fetal contraction
announces a staggering
influx of jolts

angels
winding obscurity
into a cavernous marble mind;
somewhere on earth,
a hole begins to flap
and the divided abyss
flocculates the foul table
upon which the egg
is tangled.

The voice is a hum
occasionally,
it widens
and then narrows
falters,
and then radiates
horizontally
two shores
a sea
return within reach
of physical bounds:
vague energies
protruding the dark
and floating
the floor,
          as if wheeled,

mechanical at least.

Breathing balanced the slab in the air. Soul is on every hand, this lethal silence dreaming a waning vaporous crescent heaven.

A lung is formed by walls of rotting stone. Seeming to emanate from feeble wavering beams, the lung bleeds over an array of deep damp moss through which can be distinguished rows of overgrown facades, all crumbling.

The rotting stone associates the picture of decrepitude and the signs seared into the hour have been long crescent moons of centuries.

Hollow delapidated slabs, urns repellant with rank grass and weeds suggest cavities luring the curious. Within lie catacombs, immense years nibbling the arcades of tangible refractions.

Creatures invade. High in the moon-peered valley's rim, squares peel along their edges, curling, divulging the corrosion. Herding the quicksilver.

The cranial bone. Sharpened flints. The scribbling lines across the dome are ridges of bone built up in those places where stresses occur.

This is being eaten from within. This is not a heart drumming into the table but the sound of a devouring agent located in the craw.

    Food is offered up
and eaten without chewing
swallowed violently
lending a blockade
to the torso

only the scenery changes shape

anything to detour
from what is
hurtling
to its voice.

Deeper. Entrance through the bone-branching nucleii. A digital axial nerve terminates the pulsing corticle network. A deep gorge. Foliage and granite. Coenzyme reactions underpin adrenalin rain. And here, the precipice above the ovarian diagram: veins sliding, cosmic malformations whistle. Heat.

Abruptly, the view is obfuscated, propulsion increases until the edges become blurred. Locomotion of vague origin, the altitude dips and rises, swivelling the impetus.

Velocity is haywire, maintained.

The hum splits
takes two lanes of sound
on each side of the eyes
both fast
commentary switches
from one lane to the other,
one voice
to another;
plateaus crisscrossed by
signals
showering the night
needle clear

A waterfall appears. Cartilage pumps debris through the endless cavitations. Tornadoes of the bronchioles form rain-splash contours; on grasslands, the midbrain crenellates condensed solvencies of air. Skin dribbles.

And now, absorption into the basin of a forest lake. Arteries lie dumped offshore, glowing softly. A subterranean monsoon is in full flight; here the light burns and the space is one in which everything must be repeated incessantly or be replaced.

A beach.

Someone walking, in aching deliberation towards a camera. Upon the sand beneath its seven suns, the raw tongue arranges itself into a corresponding septi-pointed crescent. Each sun is shot down by its gaze. No one outstares the seventh sun.

Arriving, the figure stoops to retrieve the convulsing flesh.

Reverse shot. Continuing, they enter the mouth of an underground cave.

Without precedent, the further the descent, the greater the originality and strangeness of events and surroundings. Words can only be formed as if the violent slipstream of an immense aerial dragnaught is vacuumed into the wide open mouth. Paralysed, the arid tongue is shoved back into itself: a lunatic worm intent on coprophilia.

Similarly, thought is experienced as a reductive process: ideas are segments stripped away from the outside of a cluster, leaving something unshelled, stripped, unrecognisable and irreducible.

```
Voice 1:   murmur in eyes
           lone murmur
           in lean zeal
           as maim,
           lunar maze,
           lame linen moan.

           moon mammal
           name isle muse
           nail in zone
           laze, lies, laze,
           loom in nominal
           milieau lamina

Voice 2:   lenses knell
           in aim liaison
           all aim
           is mean,
           manna ease,
           knees minah mane.
```

This coldness where, the heart
should be
a distant warmth amongst
more descriptive imaginings
somatic short-circuitry
outlining a figure

the line cuts under
the arm
removing the chest
an acid drip: horizontal
to the collar
corrosion
articulators
warning: flamboyance
trachea cords,
alleyways leading
out away from the centre

A tension in the back
shoulders wired
rigid
throat wrung a feeling
of drunkenness,
sensations,
connecting up
compulsions in the chest

a meter mechanised by relics
synthesis
a by-pass

because you cannot feel
you need to do this often

this,
your legacy

Even my spittle is under observation

crawl out from under the cloacal
summit
the unnerving doubt
that if I could hear this conversation
I would ever get out of it.

Gradually, imperceptibly,
the hum has developed
its dialogue
I am the witness
that is, their purpose

Everything in this space is hidden
except me.

This the inquisition. Now.

All the while, phenomena rages.

Strange perspectives lash the raw retina. Forms that span immense areas are themselves dwarfed by other forms.

A cyclone amasses shapes and these take on astonishing proportions, maliciously collapsing before the mind can grasp the tentative design.

An emotion forms
and only one:
a dark red fluid
trickling
in its visceral cage
the chest
an arabic medical text
of blood
churning in the centre
is a blackened gel
without name
isolated by
lightening, ligaments,
the bile fermenting
sluicing
at the dormancy,
contained by
phosphorescence

A climate of anxiety is dominant, as if existence itself were lying there transfixed, awaiting vivisection.

Surrounding all is a boreal distension; either it is dwelt upon, in which case there is no possibility of retreat; or, one attempts a violent wrench, a shutter action at the point where transfixation is spreading.

Awareness of the emergency of this decision becomes pain. Nevertheless, paralysis continues.

Internal bleeding
on the cutting wheels
whirring
shoved in on rods
quadrangled
bone-tight and
sapping the white blood

unflinching discs
weeping the slits

squeeze levered

climbing

Some say uncertainty begins and ends out here. A vast clearing house, humming, flashing, blinking, defies legibility of its overall design.

Here is a mirror of the stars smeared in plasma and silver. Staggered levels, platforms suspended in the haze. A system of ropeworks connect to the centrifuge tightening the trenches ; a spiral brute twisting itself deeper and higher.

Dispose the sharps, a needle is skating away at the wound. The stupor is drifting.

Dry scrapes
the last to confirm

peering
born here sighing

like a greedier grip
on the claws

of surgeons

Waking to the blue void engulfment.
Watching myself whilst also being aware
of myself watching. A telescope revolving
the ends reverting stroboscopically.
In and out. Like a muscle of spirits
being exercised.
Soaking up the anaesthesia.

Eye tapes
the first to return

hearing
cornea drying

analgesia slips
to the floor

reversants

Walls hurtling towards each other
only barely restrained from a momentous
impact. The threshold of enleashment
is the dimensions of the room. The
scavenging systems assaulted by sutures
and solutions. Awaking to the blue,
I locate myself in order to begin again.

Return to breathing, the stillness fades. With a violent heave, the rigidity is snapped and new formations begin to be habitual.

Finally, the eye can open. Immediately, the pupil inflames and burns out.

From inside the hollow circle, a larval mixture pours forth, dissolving into the atmosphere. Two nerves hotwire, a visibility takes place.

Outline a ruined cathedral
immense yet incomplete

entrance through the labyrinths:
dark openings revealed

cathedral lung
the gates of mercy

open
and then closed

and then open
both, continuously

in the same breath together

CACOPHONIES

1.

Erudition? Yes!
it's cultivated,
ventilated,
"I-the-crashed-accomplice"
a dread miserable
peopling the stars;
a dull brother,
an old shot,
a snapped barrel in the
fright bite:
a *mind*
with *a head*
of its *own*...
RRRROOWWW
C-C-C
"O tain, O tainy,
roo ca ra ca roo coo"
now riven in twain
betwixt head and toe,
between heart and foot
and whittled to this splinter,
thus fracture,
this thisness within a rupture
wherein an utterance is

balanced:

"it must be frustrating"

–mmust be mmutterance

cut up into verbiage,

the depot–fat serum plenary

heaven

of filth and oblivion,

an other–worldly bone–transmittor

scraping

below foliage:

"we can't say it,

we can't be it,

we can't *mean* it"

–it must be in here...

"it can't be said here

at all"

wrench elevator

the brute force

ignites up the clamour...

"listen neighbour,

it's becoming plastic

—here's the inside out:

a meaty hammer"

...and the jurisdiction of life

and pulp fiction about

delicious switchback

vitriol dice;

a universe of lucid dogs

GRRINDING

"I haven't read any of it yet"

and of course more winding

into a cross-section

of gases

rotating

in monochrome

and fed upon stark echoes:

"...wipes clean the yellow slates

of stars once more!"

—it's a flat contra diction

"well no, it's neither, it's just

                a piece of fiction
           and therefore nothing"
           (is represented in full)
           "or is that cohesion?"
           like the black swarm
                stares down
           into re-opening lesions;
           hungry and hatching
                for action...
"are they the brute force?"

3.

"I don't eat meat I AM meat"

-my own carcass

"you mean sarcophagus"

...contracting,

colliding...

"and the division between flesh

and celestial"

we term *thinking*

is confessed down

intentions

in fact run down

or *thisappeared*

in inking

simply piled up in tensions:

"I won't mention, I won't capture

old nothingdown..."

like steel twisted

crust crystal

galactose, digested,

arrested

in mucous spleen coprophal rings;

flash-scattering

boneyards

of fat and mucin,

old meat femur,

a neat cleavage,

the way you fracture

at the fatigue

–it's slackening:

"it's within talking distance"

4.

An omniscient solidity of air,
the outer skin
of the sphery reach
evaporated by touch
and studded into the
transmutation,
the quicksilver,
and dribbling down
the jaws of
god
yet mingling with
the warmth and greed of cells
which float among the shores
of flesh,
the slimey
firmaments
ensnared between the
jaws of carnalite
see-saws of meat;
the revolution
erratic
within the veins of clocks,
ataxia'd
and black with bursting

          -and now the sallow
             virgin doll
      is lowered onto the sky:
      the sex of god the child
               becomes
           a darkening stain
        "-in which to stare?"
         In which to stare.

5.

Clenched teeth
the soil twisted
dark vitals maimed
rocks snapping...
a head raised to the angle
of a long-range weapon;
the expiration of exhalation
and a sadist bursts forth
into foul sweet smithereens:
"and why all this violence
against language?"
–abused because innocent,
unabled
of the meaning
protruding from its neck
groping
and snapping
its way to the navel:
"what other navel can there be?"
what other *world*
but this muscle/head
hurts
along the circumnavigation
of these teeth

over

and over

in the same

twitch of the stars

operating the hideous threads

into external meatus,

malleous,

incus,

HAMMERING.

6

Eternity won't turn back
no turning in eternity;
the future's a brief case
that stands still on the table
in its brevity
as the next man in the
next ear
is about to blow up
with gas;
cursing as it slobbers up:
"thank you, I'll think that"
at ten past every sinking minute,
"the agency of enchantment
can say that"
in passed up passions
pissed on
by possible proffessed
emotions:
soul?
-it can't be grasped
like plasma trickling
through a god-sized sieve
like a parasite in paradise
in a filthy future bandage:

" you sold me to my author
when I was nearly <u>ten</u>"
... no u-turn in eternity,
eternity won't turn back:
it's a foul stomach's pearl,
"infirmity in an hour"

7

Winged
demon dimmer down
beneath skies tugging
the atavar, the atom
blur:
father son or papaboy
cauterized and slit
amongst the ganglia
for drainage
of the roly-poly ghost
cloyed and
clubbing into the life-bank;
an old penny-measurer
hacking
the anaesthetic
ashcan lipids:
"it wants to come out,
to breathe forth
–it needs to..."
there's a cadaver
advancing in the radial,
the bile vaults
breaking,
deluging

like a skeleton
but glued together from dust
and poking at the tensiles
of the earth
to help them slack
and flood:
beating at the streaming raptures
sparks
wrenched
welded
upon the dampened floors
around a sacral heart.

"like committed pedagogy
when it lit up my eyes"
—and the whites of its thighs
are infested with beeswax
and black pores
the spores of a summer's skies
"I'll never trust a man who lies"
or never trust
the oscillation between polarities
announcing life:
the struggle between blood
against algae
"you mean death?"
"I mean Satan is a selection
amongst Satans"
—it's exasperating
the harmony
into one little mention
of unreality
and then it all riddles out
like something
from the matrix world
retaining its character
but no longer matrichal:

O mol de

O mol da

So moh dah...

now populating into a forgery

a templet of poisoned sweat

founting from bottomless

indigo ancestors

that cloy in the heart:

a glutomate cohesion and dynamism

that's all a mistake

a fat stake:

it's the flavour of

con/flict

9

"I was speaking of a new concept
in conceptualisation"
–when you tied this,
this muscle
onto a cross of complex
persecution
with shards of glass
and violent yellows
–and then it went *in*
and then it went *out*
and then it
stayed out
because nothing ever happens
it always does
and then two compressed air units
swung up slightly off-key
inside here
where it's
hissing solid static
swaaassshhh
...three birds,
three urgent missive birdies
flap out from a mouth hole
dampened with acids,

like a butterfly
crawling from concrete
like a little boy
wriggling to its
death is a destination,
life a diversion,
die of a live ocean
and pray for migration.

10

Rigor mortis
unfolds a blazing claw:
"well how long is it?"
"there's only one jaw to endure
depending on how fake
we need to make it"
–or how split the listener is:
"and that's a far–fetch for anyone
to have to take it"
beginning with FISSION
or is it FUSION?
meaning
one little glimmer
in the spot of the eye
under confusion,
abrasion,
atomic head abusion;
"the void clings to this stuff"
the attraction of soporifics,
void...
rabid...
paper...
octopii;
nothing exists

it's made of articles
of vision, illusion
rabbits caper
cacophony
"in the eye of the beloved beheld"
and stuck to its own reflection
a muscular crisscross
of venom,
rejection,
only by freezing away
can it unclench
the action:
the blazing claw

11.

Paterfamilias
scratching whose blisters:
a reddish brown
liquid fat
inside a white fat
becoming blacker
by fusion
oozing inwardly
at this the incineration
of heat, hatred
and ligaments
beginning to sway
below stairs,
coagulum,
much of it dumped offshore;
a white grease coils
along the mainland
rivetting
rivulating
in the spinal horn
amongst the albumen,
the flames,
a mind screaming
and tearing at red strips,

the heat blisters,
fidgets its way
into hatred and warts;
a club swings decisively
indenting the temple
horizontally
over the ear
releasing the pressure
destruction
something tries to say,
destruction lies behind
the ear.

12

A gelatine of crushed stars
suspended
into a boiling spectrum
of crevices
and hanging by a thread of nerve,
sledgehammering
the blood, meat and bone;
the bronze columns
of a palamino machette
collapsing
hacking
the sphery platform into
four seperate planes:
heart hand and foot
but four seperate planes which
feign
to be collapsed...
fac fal
fal fac
fac fallo
it's facial, fatal,
a committed facialist
"I resist the glacialist
dock"

like money runs up the clock

pissed

as a vat of blood

slaps the head

of a vat of blood

and sledgehammers a scum surface

apotheosis

of the merely dimensional

(on four seperate planes)

in order to flight

a canopy

of glittering sidereal:

a nebular body

dragged up

from the skin pavements

like a kicked up galaxy of limbs:

"no kidding..."

13

Realitygrater,
the grated real
in the skinny stomach's greed
decaying,
faded,
submerged in *din*
but one in which the worshipful
has also been
grafted on to the
din
obliterated,
underslung,
infusioned just beneath the skin
where *being* crawls
towards a door
towards a trapdoor
towards the grated real:
a green emission
which fumigates the central
blood of the eye...
"a difficult decision
involving a matter of
lifeanddeath..."
and causing plastic caustic

leakages

shimmering through the debris,

dust,

"amongst the broken backs

of the snatched"

and sliding into glass pathways,

vegetal,

constraining,

barely anything remaining

beyond this fidget

of brainflesh

and pestilence;

clinging:

"in here or out there...

who *are* you?"

14

Entire constellations
yawn in disbelief,
terraqueous
mercurial
mundanity,
in disbelief:
"a change came over the spirit
of my dreaming..."
–in disbelief under the
sun.
Yet over the earth,
the scattered sheets of hail
obscure the saw-doctor
on fire;
the holy-marker
wobbling with grease
and shifting the poundage,
panicking:
"there is no love but me
to bring..."
Encrusted catalysis,
the fear,
the yellow fountain nightmare
curls...

the cartilage is drilled
then pinned back
and here is the hand
to squeeze the pulp
of organs dry
and here,
the breath of carrion
inflames
the torrid vista,
ruscuscitating
over and again
inside
of its own death.

15

Uncurl into catacombs
with collisions
the biters' bite
that whispers snipping
in its back
uncoiled and sprung
into the spine,
into the polished click
of hind,
yet over the echo
guitar strings clench
and rivet-in
the nether tension:
*"per me si va ne
l'etterno dolore"*
the catgut,
the musculature
cordened off, cemented
into the nape
and molded
onto the neck
and the screw;
intolerable partitions,
"per me si va ne

la citta dolente"
the light-scattering suction cup
tympani,
distension whipping the catalyst
and lashing,
twisting
the tightened contraptions,
contorted conconctions
at the end of a tether.

DEAR SURGEON

(NOTES ON VOICING)

Dear surgeon,

the operation takes place
at night
within the chancel
of a well-known cathedral:
the intention,
in physical terms,
is to approximate the conditions
occurring
under a profound freezing
surgery:
a block of concrete
houses a single vibrating reed
and this constitutes
my voice.

I have no fingers,
only a part;
a particle that is
stitched into reality
somewhere inside

approaching the root
of the tongue.

And the closer you get
to this point,
the more, that is,
that you turn back
into it
in order to taste
the very substance
of its inner marrow;
the more you realise,
or 'make real',
the finality
that this tongue
emits no language;
that it is, in fact,
an organ misappropriated
into a function
for which it never was
intended.

Those who know,
they do not speak.

> *'I cried unto god*
> *with my voice,*
> *even*
> *unto god*
> *with my voice*
> *and it gave ear*
> *unto me'*

Dear surgeon,

and how do we connect
language
up to the body?

The region of neutrality
is invaded:
proverbs,
phrases,
common scraps of knowledge,
flotsam;
all is called forth
to be subverted,
sunk,
twisted and mutilated
beyond recognition
of the recognisers
themselves:

BACKAPATAPPA
TAPPACABAPPATAK
CUKUPUT
UBAKUT
lomonos senemal
minisil
PACKATABACK
HUK

The mouth becomes
the site

at which one's
thinking
is snatched away
from its nurturance
of the heart.

In the cities,
sophisticated versions of reality
are negotiated:
communication becomes possible
but only
at those precise junctions
of meaning
which have been marked out
in advance
and worn smooth
by
a finely gritted
spittle fluid.

Switchboards, screens,
terminals,
mouths,
inevitably the friction,
the potency
of such a world
vanishes
into the midst
of its own diminishing
repetition.

And this is how

the voice
takes on the character
of an echo-sounder
in order to anticipate
the effect of an utterance
and the demand
for it,
as well as to evaluate
its distance from reality.

And for many,
this is to traverse
the entirety of their
meaning.

Like one mouth,
old sawbones,
holding another mouth
up to its
head.

And within this scenario,
this climate
of subterfuge,
the aim of the vocalist
is to exercise a muscle:
to loosen the ever-tightening
myriad
of knots
that strangle at the mouth.

First principle:
to locate and
transmit
certain signals
which have no apparent
utility
within the pre-negotiated
arenas
of meanings,
definitions,
but which, nevertheless,
conspire to articulate
that area of reality
we have selected
and retained
for ourselves
seperate
from the interactive capacity
we reach
with others:

> *Attack   it,   actuate   taut*
> *bacchic   backbite,   quack*
> *potentate   tete   a   tete   but*
> *baba   but   tiptoe   baptist*
> *putback   occupy   bite,   epic*
> *bitpart it occupy but baba...*

Somehow,
these signals,
seepages,
complete and fecund,
require externalisation;

a violent propulsion
jolting
into the startled
tongue.

And in this way,
and so forth,
the vocalist exasperates
the means by which
I
has been prised out
of its surroundings
in order that
I
may re-enter them.

In short,
one learns to name
every thing
that comes to hand
as part of one's own
existence.

Fusion occurs,
wild cross-breedings
drag us
through the nights
as definitions become
stripped of words
revenge...
and merge.

In the corner,
electricity is gnawing
at the carcass
of an infant,
wiring is everywhere,
cranium, floorboards,
heart, ceiling;
a wall is missing,
water drips onto
piles of heavy cable
dumped and soldered to the skin
of the infant carcass:
the wind wails,
the pause in eternity
is lifted.

Consider,
for the moment,
everything
upon this planet
as being a unique
tape-recording of language.
Voicing
is the physical act
which locates those signals
we choose to store
furthest
from reach of the surrounding
barrage;
that omni-mediocrity
whose purpose is to
fade
this recording
into a blur

of homogeneity.

Once located,
by transmitting these signals,
we reclaim this
uniquity:

        cobalt   object   cack   abbot
        bequest   it   kitty   pubic
        cutback...   beat   up   tactic
        but   coquette   kept   eat   it,
        kook epoxy,   optic   appetite
        at   toxic   outburst   but   pity,
        but   pity   bipartite   bouquet
        at   toxic   ubuiquity   put
        output, capitate...

        O tainny
        o tainna
        coora coo
        roo caroo
        ca roo coo
        chee ahm eeee

For my own part,
silence found me
at the age of seven
and there is more to come.
The idea of deafness,
the whole of it,
presumes a simple

loss of faith
in the sensibility
of auditory phenomena.

One may tell
of becoming a trumpet,
of something breathing
at the mouth
of a trumpet:
"I exist",
it seems to say,
"I exist
do I not?"

And so,
one simply retracts attention
from the enchanting consistency
of sound
as if to reject the viability
of such a universe
for oneself:
rejection,
stubbornness,
isolation...
—what don't you want to hear?
"Don't bother me"

Thus evolves a situation
to inhabit
voluntarily
of the spirit
and without recourse

to the body;
in my case atavistic,
a process,
a progression within
the accumulation of silence:
a valve
with which to trap
the void itself
as it is
inhaled
through the ear.

And yet,
the possibility of utterance
still hangs
inside the mouth,
poised at the site
where mind
meets body,
encircling that area
of muscle
which, most often,
is the agent of their division.

The vocalists task, then,
is to understand the act
of utterance
as a bodily function
with its attendant
mechanical dimension:
an event for its own sake
rather than simply the outcome
of a set of motivations.

To listen in
to the idiot's soul
that hops out
onto the tip of its tongue:
a piece of dynamite and swirling rope
that frosted on
to the tonsular

SAMANO-AH OAHH
SAMALLAHDAH KAMPAH
KAMPA KAMPOAH
ANCHEEEE
EEEE CHEEE
CUGH

This understanding
is best achieved
through making
a thought
both subject
and object
of itself:
to personally manifest
its invisible nature
via the physicality
of an attitude
in order to avoid
being caught
naked
within reality
but without belief in it.

Thus, the mouth becomes
the outer manifestation,
the cosmic twitchings
of an inner commitment
or lack of it.

One can say, then,
that the situation
is one of siege,
you say it:
"it is one of siege"
but still the essence
of this action
will not be seen.

This is the loop:
a universal
malevolence
pushes
at the roof of the mouth;
by applying
verbiage,
it is dislodged
but dislodged into the loop
itself:
the siege maintains
a defensive stance,
man's laughter
manslaughter,

"thou crowest into
the snare"
shit, who's
speaking?
my mouth
"I had no place to care for
for my
consider my
or hear my prayer"
"...not believe, shall not
be fatherless
he ruleth with
his JAH"
"my mouth"
shit,
who's speaking?
"for all thy worldly tongue
towards the children's
prayer
they went through
this mercy"
awash with
shit,
who's...?
its is its
our
FATUSHA
its
AKUSHLA
O deliver me
thing that pleaseth,
bring my soul onto
my soul onto
I said, I will tar O
with a bridle whirr

with thee
my heart was,
deasuggeon
my heart was,
they do not speak
my heart
dear surgeon,
heart
surgeon
they do not speak:

Those who know,
they do not speak.

Advise as to diagnosis
of complaint
indicating
appropriate operation.

yours truly.

FREEDOM, LIBERTY AND TINSEL (1989)

Existence has no exit
bulbed up on fuckout,
snapped out of exits
eviled out of I-head:
what am I even doing here?
- I found out at last;
I was an ex-It,
simply a do-nut hole torn out of the sky
through which the coming dawn
commuters form
convulsions of birds
goin'
think I'd scorch my wings??

- well I could die
just for opening my mouth
I mean speaking such shit
I mean be killed by Satan and
HIS sidekick
- I'm no buddah,
I'm a wanker:
Buddah can you spare me a dimension?
How clever. Wanker.
Or just a mention?
- upon the smooth floors of galaxies...

You see?
I have with me, at all times,
the magic words
with which to form a sentence
of death.
Of course, I can't SAY them,
they're not playthings
...I grew a flower that filled me
with tears;
feathers upon my teeth,
my nerves were sticking out HERE
far enough to form wings:
a pair of clipped and soiled
wings

that flap but never get me
in the air:

I do nothing,
I go nowhere,
I see no-one.

think I'd scorch my wings?

Everyone feeds him with brotherhood, equality, etcetera; life, experience and lights... the lullabyes, the sweetness dished up by Him We Would Dismantle... hey O shut that mouth, that suction pad, that plasticine BELIEVES. Abandon. Forty days in the desert for forty days in the here, hereafter, after HATE... the lullabyes, the bull a lies, the back of nonsense, the incense, the unsense, the incestuous nonsense with which it's made familiar. 20th Century Allergies. Nineteen solid state: like lightening, piss springs, the yellow fountain of eternities wherein everything has teeth... a transplant operation theatre error, the con text is wrought.

Don King's wild index finger, like a bludgeon thing, sits with its wild-haired blurred owner on the tip of a hotel bed waiting for tired sex action with a black nubile sweetthing of twelve years duration. Enormous, Don King's crazed hair, white sheet electric hair, outside of a boxing ring is frightening, not zany, not harmless like boxing, just frightening in a room of love, candle-lit for lovers.

Finger will be too large for the hotel's youngthing, like a sex horror blunt yellow horror sex bang blunt yellow horror bang instrument: Don King might rip wide this little slug with a tired flick, maybe.

Don King himself is too large.

This shit hole desert with its ghosts watch International Terrorism prepare to gently press the detonator as the hot breath of death blasts everything into a stomach of iron filings.

International grinned sourly, towards the viewer, towards the cactus lined horizon where the world is filled with innocent victims potentially. Like a caged animal, the frenzied air-conditioning couldn't keep from sweating. Shit hole desert. His hand, once moulded to the shape of gun metal now floats, with the purpling bruises, the innate beauty, through a wide arc in space.

Only the edge of a knife-edge of caged hysteria.

Minor car smash instant pissed blood through the windscreen as the choir broke out: something about bits of glass. Bits of glass skin snapped and peel back, cut, shot fragments of shrivelled aluminium peel back, make souvenirs with rapid yes rapid repetition into flesh bone and cartilage on the backseat where the engine has ploughed through, it sits, sprays hot black oil around the wreckage as the choir swings up a key; crunched chunks of metal take a victory kiss on impact so rapid, these lifelike masks made up from a substance called miracleflesh sell, one pint of blood each as the brain floods, going up to crescendo, cresCENDO... Hello Jamesdean.

Airport lounge hostages roam the little globe tonight. Of course they're scared, of course they know not where the next airport lounge barbaric hi-jack lounge barbarism is going to take place but they know that they are in it. They know that when the savoir fate hand was dealt, their hands contain-ed a hand-held gun held one inch from their face.

The gun contains a magazine, their faces never made the magazines on sale throughout the airport world before. These Angels flap but never once get off the floor.

Death is shaking, it is shaking in
alleyways and Paraguays, the chillin'
hands of death descend to shake the
creepin' fleas out-of-it-all: O Fol de
Rolio; like screaming through the streets
pursued by rips and cracks, the crumbling paraffinhalia of civilisation collapsing,
curling-in towards its own back: De
Rolio, no skin, no skin nor foolish
truths to hide behind, just snakes
-for-veins and flash eruptions of blood
amongst the traffic O look right: Hell
hath no fire escape; and right again:
heaven rents no step ladders... merely
a string of man-made razor blades is
tossed into the squirming pit of brotherhood, equality, etcetera...

Senator Ugly feeds in the back of his bulletproof black limousine lung thing. Feed is these small plastic bags of donated blood: feed like squirt, the Senator exists to make all his worst fears come true. Simply why he exists, just one fat worst fear bag of old paranoid blood, The Senator has a yellowing gas chamber for a heart, he says 'in one hour from now, the world will drift into the grips of delirium', things like that. Things like his liver hang from his back a-rubbing a world he would like to dismantle. His limousine carves up the landscape, the chauffeur trickling with old, sour sweat. Pouch of power Senator Ugly is fool nor lover. Abandoned, nobody hates him any more. Everyone feeds him.

For a fragment of a muscleboy:

                    like a muscle boy
               witha marrow in his bones,
                  marrow in his brains
           and many old friends from old times
                 bloody ignore that fact
            well no, actually, they sprinkled
                     in the marrow
                 one getting hugely fatter
            lost all pride and playing drums
                         fatter
                 in his marrow drinking
              and a slob gut, slob face
                  stupid bloody blame
           and his mother sucks his slob nipple
               till his heart squeezes out
                     of the marrow
                       seeping
                  through the nipple
           until the muscle boy had fell in love
                  with his own mother
              while he's living in a slob room
                cuddling with the debris
             and his own drying out heart
                  all the stink of litter
                      blown back
                    and then forth
                 and his heart persists
               and the hole in the wall
                 BELCHES the litter
           and his mother crams his heart back
                  through the nipple
              and he fucking OBJECTS
                 all of it crammed in
                        until
                  it's not a wonder
             that the muscleboy's a slob;

I should have made him necessary,
I should have made him
every bit is necessary
without a framework,
never letting even a mother
near his stupid heart.

I was in a taxi ride with Hank Williams not long ago...

It began at the Penultimate Hotel, you know, the last one before One, and I stood there in that hole of sin, screaming, kicking, soaked in gin and Hank Williams Senior stepped in talking about 'these days you can't wear your heart on your sleeve when society's wiping its nose all over your jacket.'

So I took a taxi ride with Hank Williams through the piss-wild broken night, through the desperation and the broken teeth of this Year of our Lord, Nineteen Jesus Slept.

As everyone must wear out a fool's set of tyres in their time.

Taxi! Stop. Door, get in. Could you please drive around for a while? I want to try and calm down.

And I once rode in a taxi-cab with Hank Williams and anyone could smell the after-shave upon his breath, the next step into death as songs about the fall of man and woman kind slipped out, slid down, as he slumped in his seat; just one smashed heart and a shrivelled liver hanging from his back and rubbing a world he'd like to shave off.

And he kept yelling out the window about taxi-meter time as being different from calendar time, about how finally, your just a tip of a bit of crusty toothpaste being squirted along by god-sized hands. You know? Hands across the stratosphere, taxi cabs in tubes... but I couldn't hear him.

And we both stared sullenly out the window and I began to hear the ants fucking, the moon suck sucking the earth-sick weeds towards it as fuses flashed behind my eyes and out of a new curved spine sprang glistening teeth!

And we lit this firing squad cigar.

It's a shit world! He's an heart leper said John the rat man who was driving, you know, Hank Williams is an heart leper, most his talent comes from having a heart wrapped up in chains, I mean as cold as the cold, cold snow; a stinkin' cheatin' heart that tells cold tales that tell on you...

And the doors began to pump in like meat being charred, sweat breaking out behind the chisel-featured suit of Hank Williams in another town, another show, and another radio sings 'Cry no more nor cry no less, just simply cry in the wilderness...'

As we pulled up to watch a couple in the road: Adam stuck a gun in Eve and Pulled the Universe, wiped it off, re-loaded, kissed goodbye to cheap psychology and made the crab-lice in his head foxtrot... Flump.

It was never Adam and Eve in any case, it was Adam and Steve said Hank as we drove on...

Past a supermarket selling epilepsy, one man walks in and asks for 'a strong sad sleep, I'll never get out of this world a wife.'

A tunnel appears, it seems to lead to the other side of town but doesn't, it goes deeper and down, Eve stuck her hand in my cunt and touched the tip of the pink squashed willyman, wiped a tear from its eye...

And Hank slumped deeper in his seat and sang 'I'm so lonesome that I could cry'

And I said to Hank Williams man, we've got to try and get back.

As the tunnel swerved and blew in light, where we all end up, where it all begins, in the gutter of the Penult-imate Hotel.

We were jamming nub ends even in our arteries by the time we got there.

As the fan clubs scratched and snarled against the taxi begging 'sing it Hank, just sing once more and make it all o.k. just sing it Hank and make it all, make IT all go away...'

And unitedly we sang fuck you.

We were ladelling our blood, rolling our sleeves and ladelling the blood off using syringes, winding down the windows and squirting at the citizens.

Until Hank stepped out, stepped down, lost inside the seethe and swarm of another town, another show, yeah,

I once rode in a taxi with Hank Williams not long ago. I had to pay the fare.

It was the face of god's bastard son
that shivered through my face just then
it comes!
and then it goes,
simply time-bombed out on a new sphere
of existence,
trillions of mega-zaps
per sip of tea:
it's the other face,
the other one,
petrified in oilcans
rubber and junk
so you can smell that
it is beautiful,
and it's not me!
I swear.

Everytime,
before I have to
cave your face in,
I want to kiss you.
Before I smash this, quaff! snarf!
fuck! and attack!
I want to kiss you.
It's the other one,
the face of god's bastard son
peering through carnage
bluster, dilapidation;
all that stuff,
all that shit.

I'm tired
and would have my little death-wish
with-a-bottle:
death/bottle
bottledeath
the one supports the other so
the other can be denied,

on the other side
as cool and smooth as
the flame he lives in:
I love this life, I hate this world,
I hate this world, I love this world,
love this world SO MUCH,
I just want to
schizo PHUCKOFF right OUTOF ia

The thugbaby sits in the corner
shaking the thugbaby's rattle
I mean something that feels like a
thug or a baby
or a battery of bats:
overhead
two broken nude bodies cling
to the ceiling with magnets
as the thugbaby stares
in the electric fire.
He imagines I imagine being born
in front of it,
our arms shot through
with welding rods,
copper wire,
nailed down
to the floorboards at angles,
waiting
for someone on the next floor down
with pliers...
through the ceiling;
anything.
In the meantime, the thugbaby
sees energy laugh,
laughing in the electric fire:
he is switched on,
STIFFENS.
The neighbours go out.
THUd.
One broken nude body
drops to the pulsating carpet
around the thugbaby's ears.

This was the century at its most damned:
blood stacked in penitence
did the Adam's heap
lie sprawled in gosh
on its soft-arsed back;
This is the life, they weep,
strung out on jack-plug orgies
of the sockets,
these, these eyes,
in famished packs,
push up against the checkouts
like gangs of thugs on heat
as four
damp walls
pump
long nights in.

Throughout the history of humankind,
tongues throbbed in agony,
in thistled spit,
as blurred in flesh
as the next word I break
as twice drums survival frenzy,
each filthy clotting bandage
holds in
the kingdom's discharge of the head,
now hung in nub-end bodies
it stands in the open
staggered
in the suck of a magnet sun
raised high
insisting each traditional inch:
bring on the shivering species,
that by the woven scriptures
of the sands, blah blah,
forever, on the heights,
and poor mankind in the dump heart.

O

the streets are filled with lead,
through streets of molten lead,
I walk between the heads that
grow between the pavement cracks;
hold back!
...I hear news of disaster from the
East;
news of disaster from the West,
news of disaster from all over:
bankruptcy, disaster, mmmm
squeezy fish in a town centre,
brood devourers, crazy talkers,
mouths agape for bread and germs
employing metal dragnaughts screaming
lonesome in their hell:
none would yet themselves be eaten
something needs to give
because
the streets I walk are little more
than museums of disease,
perfect piles of domicilities
packed with ghostly breath.
And your breath is nothing less
than that: Nada
nada no thing
and your dead are even less, far less,
allergic to the nub, we sup and retch
and sup and retch:
here are the first,
the last,
us final reluctant centurions,
strangest kind of swarm:
wives, molesters, rats and butterflies
mutually wounded,
we each can algebraically
make gears of progress smart:
smart on smarty
quite astonishing,
quitey quite.